Who Will Love Me?

When What You Feel Is Not Perceived As Loved

VALERIA W. STUBBS

WestBow Press books may be ordered through booksellers or by contacting:

WestBow Press
A Division of Thomas Nelson & Zondervan
1663 Liberty Drive
Bloomington, IN 47403
www.westbowpress.com
1 (866) 928-1240

ISBN: 978-1-9736-5279-3 (sc)
ISBN: 978-1-9736-5278-6 (hc)
ISBN: 978-1-9736-5280-9 (e)

Library of Congress Control Number: 2019901726

Print information available on the last page.

WestBow Press rev. date: 09/20/2019

In memory of my beloved parents,
Roosevelt Williams and
Irene Campbell Williams Juhan,
and my loving brother, Yale Wallace Perkins

CONTENTS

Introduction ix

Chapter 1: Like a Dry Ground 1

Chapter 2: I Know Him for Myself 25

Chapter 3: A Groundbreaker 39

Chapter 4: The Women's Ministry 45

Chapter 5: Jesus, Solid Like a Rock 51

Chapter 6: A Little Girl's Thirst 61

Chapter 7: Grown Woman, Little Girl 71

Chapter 8: Don't Run from the Process 79

Chapter 9: Blindsided by Inner Hurts 85

About the Author 93

Acknowledgments 95

Dedication 103

INTRODUCTION

"Always turn the hearts of the people toward me" is the commission God gave me. He is the One who truly understands and knows all things.

It is a fact that you cannot make a person love you. All your needs cannot be met by a human being. Looking for others to make you feel good about yourself is unfulfilling and miserable. When the foundation of your very existence is based on the approval and acceptance of other people, your life will be full of pain, rejection, and disappointment. Fear of rejection and disapproval can cause you to become a people pleaser, which is binding and paralyzing. *Who Will Love Me?* is based on my life experiences and the process I went through to be fulfilled. The Spirit of God taught me how to enjoy my life. It has been a journey!

As a young girl, my emotions deceived me into thinking that my dad was not my biological father based on the lack of emotional support I felt I needed from him, which he did not provide.

As a young woman, I wanted to escape life. I became suicidal, experiencing suicidal thoughts daily, but I had no definite plan of how to carry out the act. I also could not stand to look at myself in the mirror because I was uncomfortable in my own skin due to being overweight. When I accepted Jesus Christ into my life, my mind was set free of the suicidal thoughts. God answered the question of my heart, "Why was I created?" I was created to praise, to worship the Lord, and to glorify Him. Life became worth living!

During my first twelve years of salvation, the Lord taught me about His ways and His love for me. He allowed me to have insight into many under-the-surface and behind-the-scenes situations that occurred in my surroundings, which no one else seemed to see. I learned to stand alone and not follow the way of the majority. I've learned that *the majority* does not always rule and is not always right.

In the middle of a trial, the Holy Spirit whispered to me, "Judge nothing before the time," which I later discovered was a scripture (1 Corinthians 4:5 KJV). These words changed my life and my perception.

As human beings, we're prone to premature judgments and forming unfair opinions of others and their situations. We often judge people by appearance and hearsay, having bits and pieces of information but never knowing the full story.

After twelve years of walking with the Lord, I had to come face-to-face with childhood issues I never knew I had. One major issue I had to face was that I often looked to others for approval, for a sense of self-worth, and for happiness. It was clear to me that I lacked self-confidence; I felt crippled. Many times, I felt powerless under men who had strong authoritative personalities, but the longer I live, I have encountered women who have the same type of strong personality and even stronger. I knew I had rights and choices, but I did not know how to exercise these God-given privileges without the fear of displeasing those around me. I felt so insolated and overwhelmed with inner conflict by not knowing whether my perception was valid, but I knew I was entitled to my own opinions despite the surrounding voices and opinions that were louder than my own. There were times when I felt rejected and misunderstood, and often I was perceived by others as being weak and naïve.

The challenge of my many experiences was respecting the thoughts and opinions of others without doubting my own thoughts and opinions, especially when every fiber of my being gave me a different view. "God, why was I made this way? If I could just think differently!" This was the cry of my heart. I couldn't explain it. I didn't have a name for it. It's not comfortable or easy because it often puts me at odds with those around me. Often when things happen, my perception goes beyond the surface. I see the cause and the effect: the what, the when, and the how.

I've concluded, with the help of a longtime friend, that this is how God made me. Though I considered it a flaw, this insight is a gift from God. I have learned to embrace it; this gift is not just for me but for the body of Christ. I also know that people don't always want to hear my perspective because, most likely, it will go against their grain. *Oh no, here I go again,* I think when opportunities come for me to voice my opinion. I ask God for wisdom for when to say something and when to just keep my mouth shut. Have you ever been asked for advice, but after you gave it, the person became angry and refused to ask you anything else?

When God becomes our source of emotional fulfillment, we have no need to totally look to people, sex, drugs, alcohol, or our profession to meet our deepest needs.

A personal relationship with the Lord is irreplaceable, and He supplies all our needs. His grace is sufficient!

Even on our best days, because we are human, we may hurt and let people down. However, as long as we live, we cannot escape getting hurt and being disappointed. The Word of God says that "offences will come" (Luke 17:1 KJV). "For it must need be that offences come" (Matthew 18:7 KJV).

I thank God for forgiveness and for the ability to let go. My love walk (living like God instructs in His Word) is still being perfected in me daily. It is truly a process because the war between living in the flesh or walking in the Spirit is a daily battle.

Throughout this book, I will be sharing little nuggets that the Holy Spirit has taught me about people and much more. I am now enjoying my life because of my journey, yet I'm ever learning. I am looking unto God for bigger and better things. I pray that the wisdom given to me will help make your life more enjoyable as well. All the glory and honor belong to God. I thank Him for all the people and the lessons learned that have helped me get to this point. "The steps of a good man are ordered by the Lord: and he delighted in his way" (Psalm 37:23 KJV).

CHAPTER 1

Like a Dry Ground

Many people spend most of their lives being angry, complaining, and crying about what their mothers, fathers, sisters, brothers, spouses, children, in-laws, bosses, and coworkers have done to them. I'll go as far as to include their crying and complaining about the pain the church has caused them—whether it was caused by church members, bishops, pastors, deacons, or any other person in leadership.

Yes, the pain you feel may be real and justified. It happened—whatever it may be—but what are you going to do about it now? How long are you going to let past or present situations hold you captive? How long will you be held prisoner, held in confinement? Being a prisoner of circumstances is a soul-wrenching condition, and you need inner healing.

Five sure warning signs of a need for inner healing are as follows: (1) Reliving the situation repeatedly in your mind. (2) Expressing to everyone how hurt you are and how unfairly you were treated. Unintentionally, your conversation ends up on the situation; it just spews out of your mouth. (3) Feeling angry every time you see the individual(s); you still feel the pain as if it happened yesterday. (4) Refusing to develop new relationships out of fear of being hurt again. (5) Comparing every situation or person to your previous incident. You may feel that all people—men, women, children, and Christians—are alike, but I have learned they are not.

It's time to let it all go and forgive all those who have hurt you so that you can begin your healing process. If you choose to hold on to your hurts, you will go into survival mode, building walls and barricading yourself into your own little guarded world. The consequence of your choice will keep old baggage in and new and exciting experiences out of your life due to your determination that no one will ever hurt you again. Don't underestimate the power of God or the influence of the devil.

Regardless of what you have gone through in your family, on your job, in your relationships, and even in the church, there are still some sincere, honest, and loving people, pastors, and leaders who fear God. They are not perfect, and neither are you. You need to pray for others and stay focused on God. There are still marriages that endure the test of time. There are families determined to stick together from generation to generation. Lifelong friendships are still treasured. And believe it or not, there are companies that understand the importance of valuing their employees and holding management accountable for how it treats people, and they don't spare any expense. I admire churches that also utilize this powerful tool of ongoing leadership training through workshops and seminars. I believe an important attribute of a leader is having people skills. Most people are not naturally born with this skill. It minimizes hurts and wounds inflicted on people due to a lack of training, especially in the church.

Life is too short, and the world and its entire splendor are too great, to allow hurtful situations to hinder you from enjoying your life. Think about it. Our God is an awesome God! He is ready, able, and willing to give us wisdom, knowledge, understanding, and direction in our lives.

Questions: What are you going through—or have you gone through—that you can honestly say hinders you from moving forward in your life? What scenario keeps playing over and over in your mind? You can't let it shut you down, but you can grow from it, whether it's your fault or not. I understand there is a grieving process in many situations. You have cried over it, prayed about it, and experienced many sleepless nights trying to figure out why. You have concluded that you cannot make sense of it. Now make a decision to get up.

I have learned to use every hurt as a stepping-stone. Hurtful situations made me sensitive to the hurts of others. Talking about your hurts to a person in confidence for healing purposes is only one part of the healing process. Then a decision must be made on your part; the way out is by letting go and forgiving.

Forgiveness is the key—the necessary ingredient to being free. Jesus is our prime example of forgiveness. He was misunderstood, spit on, beaten, mocked, and denied. While hanging on the cross, Jesus said, "Father forgive them; for they know not what they do" (Luke 23:34 KJV).

Therefore, Jesus knew what was in humankind, and people did not have a true understanding of what they were doing. Jesus knew why He came into this world.

He also knew what He would endure at the hands of humankind. While in the garden of Gethsemane, He prayed, "O My Father, if it is possible, let this cup pass from Me: nevertheless, not as I will, but as You *will*" (Matthew 26:39 NKJV).

There will be times we want the cup of trials to be taken from us; be assured you are not alone. If Jesus forgave, we can do it also. It is not going to be easy because some wounds have a stronger impact than other wounds. But you can forgive and move on with the Lord's help. Do not waste time expecting an apology or an explanation from the person(s) who hurt you. I believe some issues can be cleared up with just good, old-fashioned communication. However, we are not all good at that skill, and sometimes the others involved are simply not willing to have open and honest communication about the situation, even for the main purpose of peace, understanding, reconciliation, and restoration. Some people are unwilling to confront unpleasant issues and want to feel right at any cost. "All the ways of a man are clean *and* innocent in his own eyes [and he may see nothing wrong with his actions], but the Lord weighs *and* examines the motives *and* intents [of the heart and knows the truth]" (Proverbs 16:2). Make a choice to forgive, and let your offenders go so that you can be free.

Staying before the Lord in prayer and reading the Word of God are our greatest weapons in tough situations. Applying the Word of God mixed with faith where we hurt is a healing salve to one's hurting soul. One of the most important steps in overcoming an unforgiving attitude is focusing your attention on how much God has forgiven you.

We should not take God's forgiveness for granted, especially when we withhold our forgiveness from others. As a result, we behave as though others' sins against us are more serious than our sins against God.

Many people who have caused hurt have moved on with their lives. Some of them are not the same people anymore because time does bring about change. Life has a way of teaching us lessons, and we all have a course to run. I love the following scripture:

> And forgive us our debts, as we have forgiven our debtors [letting go of both the wrong and the resentment]. And do not lead us into temptation, but deliver us from evil. [For Yours is the kingdom and

> the power and the glory forever. Amen.] For if you forgive others their trespasses [their reckless and willful sins], your heavenly Father will also forgive you. But if you do not forgive others [nurturing your hurt and anger with the result that it interferes with your relationship with God], then your Father will not forgive your trespasses. (Matthew 6:12–15)

I always ask the Lord to forgive me of my sins—the ones I know about and the ones I am not aware of—because none of us have made it yet. This world is full of imperfect people, including you and me. All of us have issues at some level; we need God. It amazes me when I hear people make statements about how they have been hurt and rejected by people, but they do not have a clue or have forgotten the pain and rejection they have inflicted on others. Before we criticize what someone else is doing, let's take a good look at ourselves.

I ask the Lord to help me not hurt people like I have been hurt or like I have seen people get hurt. I say this humbly because the potential to do so is in me also. The next time you cry about what someone has done to you, think about what you have done. Then maybe the struggle to forgive will not be so difficult.

I went through a very painful situation with a sister in the Lord. I felt rejected, cut off, and separated. Our relationship changed, and I did not know why she was distant. I went to her several times to find out what was going on. I even asked her to please forgive me if I had offended her in any way. Each time I was told I had not done anything. That was all she would say, which still left me hanging. I just could not understand the change in our relationship.

I later learned how that friend had gone through something she couldn't share with me, and it had nothing to do with me. She had dealt with a very difficult issue. After it was over, I expected my friend to say, "I'm sorry for the pain I caused you," but she never did. I realized that she did not know what I experienced through the entire situation. If she had said, "I'm going through something right now, and I cannot talk about it. Just pray for me," I would have accepted her statement and allowed her some space. But she did not. She handled things the best way she knew how to handle them. It would have saved me from getting hurt, but, on the other hand, if it had not happened, I would not have gained the experience and knowledge that I did. I would not be the person I am today.

Psalm 119:71 says, "It is good for me that I have been afflicted (in pain or suffering, troubled), That I might learn your statutes (your laws)." During times of affliction like these, God taught me the laws of love and forgiveness. The lesson learned was that when changes happen in a relationship, sometimes it has nothing to do with you.

First John 4:7–8 (NKJV) says, "Beloved, let us love one another: for love is of God; and everyone who loves is born of God and knows God. He who does not love does not know God; for God is love." As Christians, love is more than talking; it is actions. In other words, we must demonstrate it. The Lord has a way of showing us what is in us, and sometimes He uses situations to deliver us from the harmful patterns we have developed throughout our lives. I was forced to take a good look at myself. How could I allow another person's actions to affect me in such a manner until I was miserable and sad? I felt so empty, and I was convinced that I had done something wrong for her to be so distant from me.

My healing process started with prayer. I had two friends who saw my tears of pain, and we spent two days praying to God at one of their homes. After prayer, my friends and I sat on the floor and talked about the hurts and the times we had felt rejected. We did not spend time blaming people and calling names; instead, we talked about the rejection we had experienced. We discussed the image we had of ourselves as young girls, which was the real issue.

Those two days of prayer were very powerful, rewarding, and life changing for me. Ephesians 6:12 (KJV) says, "For we wrestle not against flesh and blood, but against principalities, against powers, against the rulers of the darkness of this world, against the spiritual wickedness in high places." I thank God for that painful situation because it was the beginning of a new chapter in my life. It started a shift in me, bringing me to a new level of growth and maturity. It brought an inner healing to me *and* to them. I began to search the scriptures for answers to questions such as, "How do I move from feeling like a victim into being victorious?"

I found Mark 11:25, which says, "And whenever you stand praying, if you have anything against anyone, forgive him [drop the issue, let it go], so that your Father who is in heaven will also forgive you your transgressions *and* wrongdoings [against Him and others]."

The Spirit of God helped me through this ordeal. He taught me how to be at church, see my friend, and still function without being overtaken by hurt. This was a difficult time for me because I felt disconnected from everyone. My emotions were going crazy, yet I had to keep going.

I had to learn how to be comfortable with myself in a crowded room. I felt weird and abnormal at times. On my way to church, I would comfort myself by saying, "You are going to be okay" and "If you see her, smile and wave." I knew I had to go through it, even though it was uncomfortable. After church, I spoke, hugged, and laughed with people while making my way to my car and leaving with a sigh of relief. I realized my problem was not with the people; the battle was within me.

Thankfully, it has been years since all of that happened, and our friendship was not lost. Look at how God took a situation such as this to show me how dependent I was on her to make me feel good about myself. God will reveal to us what is in us, and through His love for us, He is able to deliver us from any unhealthy boundaries in relationships or issues.

Questions: What has happened in your life that you might need to take a second look at? What is the lesson you can learn about yourself when faced with hurtful and uncomfortable issues in relationships? Think about it! Warning: The temptation will come at times to get angry and build up walls by developing an "I don't care" attitude with the person(s) you are experiencing issues with. This is a way of protecting yourself from getting hurt, which is not good. Even though I thank the Lord for that experience, looking back on it now, I could have handled the situation in a more mature way. I should have gone into prayer for her from the beginning, but I did the total opposite. I was more concerned about myself.

There will be times when you may hurt a person unknowingly and they may pull back from you, and if that is the case, you should go to that person and make it right by investigating the situation. Ask them if you have offended them in some way, and if you have, ask for forgiveness.

It is difficult for some people to expose their true feelings or admit they were hurt or angry for several reasons: (1) They have not reached the level of maturity to effectively confront issues. (2) They experience fear of rejection. (3) They feel shame. (4) They feel unsafe and vulnerable. (5) They fear that their perspective and feelings will not be honored, respected, or considered valid. (6) They fear a backlash, making things worse, or blowing things out of proportion. (7) Pride. It is easier to cut people off, speak badly of them, and become distant when relationships go sour, which is not a healthy pattern. (8) They just do not want a relationship with you anymore.

A word to the offended person: You are doing yourself a great injustice by not telling a person what they have done to hurt you. The offender will continue to hurt you if you do not tell them. You cannot worry about the response. You must free yourself, and you have that right. James 5:16 (KJV) says, "Confess your faults one to another, and pray one for another, that you may be healed. The effectual fervent prayer of a righteous man availeth much."

I hope the injured person will respond honestly and respectfully, but if he or she refuses to acknowledge and talk about your concerns, continue to pray for them. Ask God to forgive you if you have hurt that person, but do not get stuck! I have learned that some folks change relationships like they change clothes. When they have no more use for you, they move on and latch on to someone else until something happens. I had to face the fact that some folks are not stable; they do not know how to be in or keep a relationship. Do yourself and them a favor: forgive them, forgive yourself, and move on graciously.

You cannot force a person to open up and talk to you. You cannot force a person to forgive you and continue a relationship with you. Consider this: maybe the relationship you thought you had was not healthy in the first place. Sometimes separations in a relationship allow space for reconstruction. Take note: what we say and do during a separation can make reconciliation easy or almost impossible.

"A brother offended *is harder to win* over than a fortified city, and contentions [separating families] are like the bars of a castle" (Proverbs 18:19). After you have done all you know to do, pray for the peace of God. "Be anxious for nothing, but in everything by prayer and supplication, with thanksgiving, let your requests be made known to God; and the peace of God, which surpasses all understanding, will guard your hearts and minds through Christ Jesus" (Philippians 4:6–7 NKJV).

Certain ingredients are important for creating and maintaining healthy relationships. Healthy relationships must have the ability to confront issues when necessary and have open and honest communication. They must allow their friends space to grow into their own destiny, thereby creating mutual respect, integrity, and honor. Other ingredients in a healthy relationship are sharing your friends with others and allowing them the freedom to develop other friendships that you may not be a part of. I believe destroyers of healthy relationships are sometimes controllers and manipulators, which seek to dominate the outcome of situations so that things can always go their way. An unhealthy relationship disregards the choices of others by not allowing them the freedom to say yes or no without guilt and repercussions.

Beware of the expectations and demands you impose on those around you due to your own unhealthy inner issues and inner needs. Do not put demands on anyone beyond their limits—just to stay in your good graces.

The desire to be loved is natural, and, depending on our experiences, we learn to cope with life the best way we know how. This coping mechanism can cause us to develop unhealthy patterns to get the results we want, which is to be loved.

Questions: Will you agree with me that some patterns you have developed are harmful? What are your patterns when people do not do what you expect them to do? Do you put them down and pick up someone else? Are you a user? After all, you want what you want. Do you try to teach people a lesson to prove that you do not need them? Do you ignore them or give them the cold shoulder as a way of punishment and to show them your disapproval? Are you stubborn and headstrong? Why do you do the things you do? Why do you say the things you say? Could it be for revenge? Do you justify your attitude by saying, "You said it to me, so I'll say it to you"? Do you have problems with jealousy? Do you try to make yourself look good while making others look bad; in other words, do you throw people under the bus? Can you be honest with yourself about you? Why do you refrain from giving to others what you desire (affirmation, compliments, forgiveness, mercy, and grace)?

What words do you long to hear, but you never seem to hear? Is it, "Great job," "I knew you could do it," "I love you," "You are the best, "I know I can count on you," "You are a great friend," "You are a great sister," "You are a great brother," "You are a great father," or "You are a great mother"?

Now it is your turn to pause and take a few moments to think about it. What are the words you desire to hear? From whom do you desire to receive affirming words? Is it your boss, teacher, children, husband, or wife? Could it be your parents, coworkers, or church family? If you are a pastor, what do you long to hear from your church members? Some of these people mentioned above are very important to us, and their opinions mean everything. If they do not say the words you desire, will you feel disappointed, unimportant, rejected, hurt, empty, unloved, unappreciated, lonely, and worthless?

Confront your thoughts now. Who are you blaming for your dry ground? Sometimes people will withhold love and refuse to say affirming words to you because they know you want it. People will give and take away. Strangely enough, these same people feel they are worthy and deserving of and will demand the very thing they refuse to give you. Take back the power you have put into another person's hand—the power to control how you feel and think about yourself. You cannot build your hopes and confidence in humanity; what you need is dependency on the Lord.

Have you ever noticed the ground when it is extremely dry due to a lack of rain for a long period of time? When a normal rain comes, the ground dries quickly, and surprisingly, there is no sign that it ever rained. Due to the deficiency of water, the whole environment will suffer—the animals, the plants, and the people—because they depend on the land to survive. Just like dry ground in need of water, we can forever thirst for love, validation, acceptance, and approval and never get enough of what we feel we need to satisfy our thirsty souls. The soul is the invisible part of us, and it is the part that perceives, reflects, feels, and desires. The Lord is the Healer of our thirsty souls. We can go to him unashamed and ask for help.

> Return, O Lord, rescue my soul; Save me because of Your [unfailing] steadfast love *and* mercy. (Psalm 6:4)

Looking back over my life, I was so thirsty for love, acceptance, approval, and validation. Even though I didn't know it at the time, I developed unhealthy behavioral patterns. As a young woman, before I accepted Jesus into my life, when my boyfriend and I were together, I pretended to have fainted. His response made me feel so good and special. Imagine when he jumped up in excitement, patted my face, shook me, and called my name, "Valeria! Valeria! Valeria!" Then, I slowly woke up. It was strange, but his reaction gave me some kind of gratification and fulfillment. After that episode, I decided I would not do that again because it was nothing but manipulation. I believed it was the Lord who made me recognize the reason why I did that. Being honest with myself, it was to get attention.

Questions: What have you done for attention? Just how far have you gone to get what you want? Come on, think about it! Self-examination is not easy. It is ugly, painful, and messy. It causes us to look inside of ourselves, and we are not always pleased with what we see. It is easier to look at another person's faults than to look at our own. To what extent will you go to make yourself look good just to be liked and accepted? Who are you purposely manipulating, controlling, and punishing by not talking to them? Do you, yourself, feel controlled and manipulated? What is going on inside of you?

I am convinced that we cannot depend on others to make us feel good about ourselves. Accepting this truth will start the healing process. We can begin to build our self-esteem by taking steps to improve our self-image. First, adapt a new attitude about loving yourself. Take an inventory of your gifts and talents that God has placed within you and then embrace and celebrate them! "I will give thanks *and* praise to You, for I am fearfully and wonderfully made; Wonderful are Your works, and my soul knows it very well" (Psalm 139:14).

Honestly, look at yourself and your surroundings and have the courage to make some positive, cost-effective changes: pamper yourself, get a manicure and pedicure, try a new hairstyle, buy a new outfit, or change your environment by rearranging one or more rooms in your home. Investigate your community, join a fitness center, find an organization that offers classes that pique your interest, such as arts and crafts, drawing, painting, pottery, crocheting, Spanish, jewelry techniques, wood carving, sign language, swimming, sewing, or piano. Join a Toastmasters group or a book club. These are ways to discover unknown talents and gifts and meet new and positive people.

The hunger for love and happiness can lead us into dangerous territories. Filling our empty places with temporary fixes can be a matter of life or death, joy or sadness.

If you want a life filled with true love, lasting joy, and happiness, it begins with accepting Jesus Christ into your heart. The plan of salvation is not complicated. You must believe that you are a sinner and in need of a Savior:

> For all have sinned and come short of the glory of God. (Romans 3:23 KJV).

> That if thou shalt confess with thy mouth the Lord Jesus, and shalt believe in thine heart that God hath raised him from the

> dead, thou shalt be saved. For with the heart man believeth unto righteousness; and with the mouth confession is made unto salvation. (Romans 10:9–10 KJV)

> For whosoever shall call upon the name of the Lord shall be saved. (Romans 10:13 KJV)

> If you want to receive Jesus as your Lord and Savior, repent of your sins and ask Him to come into your life. Father, in the name of Jesus, I know that I am a sinner. I ask you to forgive me of my sins. I believe that your Son, Jesus Christ, shed His blood on the cross and died for my sins and that you raised Him from death to life. Lead and guide me in the path you will have me to go in Jesus name. Amen

Questions: What price will you pay to feel love, satisfaction, or fulfillment from another person? Just how far will you go and what will you sacrifice just to say, "I have experienced this thing called love," as we know it?

Many have sacrificed their families, their jobs, even their reputations for a moment of pleasure. We can lose our self-worth by allowing people to trample over us emotionally, mentally, and physically, stooping low to keep people in our lives by giving our bodies away to someone to prove our love for them. Everyone needs love; there is not an age limit to this God-given desire. However, using ungodly things to fill the voids in our lives can be costly to our souls.

Admittedly, I desperately wanted to feel loved and connected to someone, which caused me to sacrifice my own self-love. Many times, the sex was painful, the moans and groans were not from pleasure but from the accompanying pain, and I wanted the act to be over. I didn't have enough self-love to say, "Stop!" I endured the physical pain, and they walked away satisfied, thinking they had done something great. I felt used and abused, yet I allowed it.

Warning: God's Word clearly warns us of the danger of committing adultery and fornication.

> Run away from sexual immorality [in any form, whether thought or behavior, whether visual or written]. Every *other* sin that a man

> commits is outside the body, but the one who is sexually immoral sins against his own body. (1 Corinthians 6:18)

There are diseases out there that will cost you everything—your life and everyone connected to you. We are living in a day where married couples are blessed when they have a faithful husband or wife. We are also living in a day where virgins are rare. Sexually transmitted diseases are real. People diagnosed with sexual diseases comes in all sizes, shapes, and colors. I am warning you that one night, one slipup, or being in the wrong place at the wrong time can turn into a nightmare. One candlelight dinner date, which seems harmless with nice romantic music playing in a private and compromising setting, can be a setup for sin and death—both spiritual and physical. One innocent compliment and one heart-to-heart conversation can change your whole world. Consequently, there are many traps awaiting married and single individuals who are wrongly focused. Do not confuse gratification and lust with love! True love can wait. It is built on godly values, trust, and honest communication.

We do not know real love and cannot recognize real love until we have experienced the unconditional love of God first.

> This is My commandment, that you love *and* unselfishly seek the best for one another, just as I have loved you. No one has greater love [nor stronger commitment] than to lay down his own life for his friends. (John 15:12–13)

When God created us, He made a special place reserved just for Him in our hearts. Only His love can fulfill our deepest emotional needs.

CHAPTER 2

I Know Him for Myself

I feel the best advice I can give to a new Christian and remind an older Christian of is how important it is to be connected to a body of Bible believers. Ask and trust the Lord to lead you to a church where you can grow in Him spiritually. Get a good study Bible and submerge yourself in the Word of God. Ask the Lord for wisdom, knowledge, and understanding. Develop a prayer life because, believe me, you are going to need it. Coming out of the streets, leaving your old way of living, and walking into a newness of life will be a journey.

> Let us seize *and* hold tightly the confession of our hope without wavering, for He who promised is reliable *and* trustworthy *and*

> faithful [to His word]; and let us consider [thoughtfully] how we may encourage one another to love and to do good deeds, not forsaking our meeting together [as believers for worship and instruction], as is the habit of some, but encouraging *one another*; and all the more [faithfully] as you see the day [of Christ's return] approaching. (Hebrews 10:23–25)

In the church, you will learn how to put the Word of God into action. You will learn about the character of God and how to display His character. We are not born with godly character. But after accepting Him as Lord and Savior, through God's Word, and by having an intimate relationship with Him, we learn how to pray and exercise our faith. We learn about grace and loving unconditionally. We learn how to love our husbands or wives and our children. We learn to forgive—even our enemies. We learn how to get along with people, how to settle disagreements, and how to follow leadership as they follow Christ. The benefits are great, and instructions and directions for your life are given. In Christ we can have peace, joy, hope, comfort in trying times, and so much more.

That is what I learned and experienced during the first twelve years of my salvation. Everything I have been through in Christ has made me who I am today. My first pastor instilled in me, "If you don't have love, you don't have God." And if you walked in any level of victory, it is by His grace and through the power of God that we maintain our level of victory. I was taught that the Holy Spirit would lead and guide us into all truth and to be real with ourselves because there is no good thing in this flesh. Through many spiritual trials, the Holy Spirit taught me many valuable lessons that will never be forgotten.

When I was young, we had a piano at home, and I played the piano a little by ear. When I joined the church, they didn't have a musician, so I became the church organist. The church welcomed me with open arms, and they treated me like I was a professional. Although I had room for improvement, my talent was considered a great addition to the services. There was one tune for shouting and one tune for the congregational songs with different words.

As the church continued to develop, more songs were added, and the choir was formed. I struggled and wanted to take the choir to another level, so my pastor and I agreed to hire a musician to play for the choir. She said, "Watch the new musician play, but be discreet in your observation because she might play in such a way that it might be hard for you to pick up some pointers from her playing." I obeyed, and that was when I encountered my first trial in the church.

One night before choir rehearsal, the musician and I were at the church alone, and I was standing beside her, admiring and watching her play. Out of nowhere, she looked up at me and said, "You don't have to be jealous."

I said, "Jealous? I'm not jealous."

She continued to play, and I felt something was not right about that woman. I was still a babe in Christ, and I did not understand what was going on. The only way I knew how to handle the accusation was to just observe the woman and stay prayerful. I became a little distant and quiet, and maybe it was noticeable.

She taught us several songs for at least two weeks, and finally we were going to sing during a Sunday service. I asked if I could take the music sheets home to study the words because I had trouble remembering the words, and I promised to bring the sheets back for the soloist.

Well, Sunday came, the praise service was ending, and it was almost time for the choir to sing. I went into a panic, rushed to the back, and beckoned for one of the sisters to come. I told the sister to tell the soloist that I had left the music at home by mistake.

The sister came back with a response that blew me away. The soloist had said, "Oh, she's just jealous."

I was so hurt that the choir did not sing because the soloist needed the words to the song. Immediately after the service, I went to the musician to explain what had happened. Boy, did she let me have it, saying I was jealous and accusing me of leaving the sheets at home on purpose. Most of the church believed I was jealous—maybe because of the change in my demeanor. I wanted to defend myself, but the Holy Spirit told me it was one of the times I had to rest in the Lord, knowing that He knew the truth.

Later on that Sunday night, I received a call from my pastor stating that the woman was not coming back to play for us and asking me to apologize to the musician. I explained what had happened, but she still asked me to apologize.

I submitted to her request. I did it for the sake of peace.

> Follow peace with all men, and holiness, without which no man shall see the Lord. (Hebrews 12:14 KJV)

> Obey those who rule over you, and be submissive, for they watch out for your souls. (Hebrews 13:17a NKJV)

When I called the woman and apologized, she said, "What are you apologizing for?"

I said, "For causing you to feel that I am jealous."

She accepted it, but she never came back to the church to help us.

Later, I had a chance to explain what had happened in more detail to my pastor.

After that trial, I asked the Lord during prayer, concerning the whole ordeal, "What was that?"

His statement to me was, "That was your first spiritual warfare."

That trial had a major impact on me; regardless of how things appear, it doesn't make things true. I had to stand alone, knowing that God knew the truth—even if my church family and pastor did not.

I sat through many messages fashioned just for me. Was that right? No! However, that is the human side of people, which includes pastors and other people in authority. I kept my spirit right with my pastor by not getting an attitude with her and not allowing my heart and mind to be polluted with confusion, anger, and resentment.

There will be times when you will suffer unfair treatment as I suffered. I am a witness. Tell God about it, and He will fight your battle. I learned to rest in the Lord (trust and stand still, not to move) from my place in the ministry during and after that trial because I had the Lord on my side. He had my back!

That is why you need to know the Lord for yourself. The Lord will allow you to experience many things in the church—some good and some bad—but it is how you handle and react to them that matters most. The devil's intention is to get us out of the church, being afraid to commit ourselves to a body of believers, and most of all, he wants to lead us away from God. There are so many hurting people sitting at home and in churches because of bad experiences. Get to know the Lord. There is no perfect church with perfect people in it.

> Consider it nothing but joy, my brothers and sisters, whenever you fall into various trials. Be assured that the testing of your faith [through experience] produces endurance [leading to spiritual maturity, and inner

> peace]. And let endurance have its perfect result *and* do a thorough work, so that you may be perfect and completely developed [in your faith], lacking in nothing. (James 1:2–4)

Trials of any sort and various temptations can be some of your most difficult times. During these times, it is important to have the Holy Spirit. He is your Comforter, Leader, and Guide. Because of my experience, I am not easily moved by other people's perceptions and opinions because things are not always what they appear to be. Even though the majority says it is right, that does not mean it is always right.

I learned that when people do not understand, God does, and when people do not know my whole story, God knows. I learned that human understanding is limited, but God's knowledge and understanding are unlimited. People might miss the mark, but God gets it right every time. People might not want to hear my story, but God will listen. People will disappoint at times, due to human shortcomings and limitations, but God is faithful. Most of all, I know that human love is conditional, but God loves me unconditionally. What an awesome God!

The Holy Spirit taught me many things I did not understand. As a babe in Christ, I knew only what I was taught, and I was comfortable with that. I was not searching for any new revelations apart from my pastor's teaching. You need to understand the era that I was in. A lot of traditional things were taught, and many times during Bible study, the Spirit of God whispered to me and said, "Go home and study because what you are hearing is not rightly divided." My questions to the Lord were, "How could this be, and why me?" I thought, *If the man or woman of God said it, it must be right.*

One night, I literally shut my Bible and said, "No! No! I'm not ready for this," hoping the nudging would go away. I became weary of the Holy Spirit prompting me to study God's Word for clarity. It was not with a self-righteous motive, purposely looking for words that were different from my pastor's teaching. Despite my feelings, I could not ignore the promptings any longer. I finally gave up and stopped fighting. I said, "Okay! Okay! I give up. Show me."

One of the things I studied for myself was the wearing of jewelry. Back in the day, the wearing of jewelry was considered worldly, and it was associated with Jezebel.

> The wall was made of jasper, and the city of pure gold, as pure as glass. The foundations of the city walls were decorated with every kind of precious stone … The twelve gates were twelve pearls, each gate made of a single pearl. The great street of the city was of gold, as pure as transparent glass. (Revelation 21:18–21 NIV)

I thought, *If all this valuable stuff is in heaven, why can't we wear it here on earth?* Because of my study, I realized that there is nothing wrong with wearing jewelry. Despite all that, I knew my pastor's heart and intention. My pastor at the time wanted all of us to live holy lives. She was sincere about the Word of God and preached it according to her understanding.

The Lord informed me that what He revealed to me was for my learning only. I did not go through the congregation telling what the Lord shared with me. I kept what I learned to myself; those truths were for me and for my understanding. The Lord will not share *hidden* truths with a foolish person because such a person can do more damage in a church than good. I dared not be lifted up in my flesh, thinking I was above the pastor because, in fact, those were frightening times in my life. Can the Lord trust you with unspoken truth—truth about a situation or a circumstance that seems so real to those around you?

In those days, the Word of God was taken out of context because of church doctrine and traditions. My pastor always said, "It is important that we know the Word of the Lord for ourselves." This is a powerful concept: know the Lord for yourself. Wow! Talk about a confident and courageous pastor! Hold on to your hats.

During a revival consisting of several evangelists, one of them preached against the television, which he referred to as the one-eyed monster. He preached so strongly about the one-eyed monster that I wanted to get that one-eyed monster out of my house. What people believe, whether it is right or wrong, they stand strongly for or against.

After that fiery sermon, I went home to get my brand-new, thirteen-inch color television—not black and white—and a hammer. I took them near the dumpster up the street. One of the sisters from the church wanted to take part in destroying my one-eyed monster. I raised my hammer in the air and hit the television screen three times: one for the Father, one for the Son, and one for the Holy Spirit. The sister who accompanied me took the hammer and hit what was left of my television—my one-eyed monster. Yes, one for the Father, one for the Son, and one for the Holy Spirit. Then she went home to her television.

Later that week, I visited my pastor's home, and she was watching television (the one-eyed monster) and eating ice cream. I sat down with her, looking the opposite direction of the television and thinking that something was wrong with that picture. Reality set in, and I thought, *I've been duped. I'm living alone in a big house without a television.*

The greatest mistake I made was that I should have talked to my pastor to get clarity regarding the one-eyed monster message. She didn't teach against the television and did not know what I was going to do that night. I ended up calling the neighborhood television repairman to repair a big old black-and-white television I had that sounded like thunder if you hit the sides of it. What an experience! It is funny now, but it was not funny then. I needed understanding. We learn about the Lord through our experiences. I acquired some wisdom that day. "Happy is the man that findeth wisdom, and the man that getteth understanding" (Proverbs 3:13 KJV).

It takes time in the Word and prayer and experience to recognize the voice of the Lord. "My sheep hear My voice, and I know them, and they follow Me" (John 10:27 NKJV).

In the church where I learned to serve (work in a ministry), I was the organist, a church van driver, and the children's Sunday school teacher. I sang on the praise team and cleaned the church. I was also the aide and nurse to my pastor when needed, especially during her extended days of fasting and prayer.

There is no perfect pastor or perfect church because imperfect people are in the church. In the church and out of the church, the Lord allowed me to experience many things—some very tough and rewarding things. I have been misunderstood, misjudged, falsely accused, and gossiped about. I've suffered loss of relationships and material things, but I have also gained. I've made mistakes and have fallen, but I have gotten up. I've been hurt and have unintentionally hurt others, but I have forgiven others and have been forgiven. I know about depression and suicidal thoughts, but now I am loving life. Despite it all, I am determined to enjoy this life that Jesus died for me to live abundantly. "It is good for me that I have been afflicted; that I might learn thy statutes" (Psalm 119:71 KJV).

We all have strengths and weaknesses. Many of us who were saved years ago, or even recently, have stories to tell simply because of the unspoken dynamics in the church (all the forces that are at work in a church). All churches have their dynamics, which is not a bad thing, although it is not always good either.

One of the dynamics of a church may be traditions: passed-down behaviors, thought processes, attitudes, and views from one leader to another. The roots, the foundation of a church, will explain the church's dynamics. If the Lord calls you into your own ministry, take the good that you have learned and leave the bad. Pray for wisdom because some traditions need to be left in the past and some need to be kept, which is why we need the guidance of the Holy Spirit. We need wisdom, knowledge, and understanding. I thank God for my foundation, and I must admit that there are times even now when the Holy Spirit reminds me not to forget the things I have learned because that is how I am able to stand during difficult times in every area of my life. Experiences and tough times will season you and anoint you for service.

Questions: What is my story? Have I grown from my many experiences? Am I better or bitter? Have I made peace and forgiven all past hurts? Am I growing in the Lord—or is my growth stunted? Only you can answer these questions.

CHAPTER 3

A Groundbreaker

My definition of a groundbreaker is simply a person doing something new that is not normally done. A groundbreaker can cause a change in the world, in the home, in relationships, in the workplace, or in the church. Their courage paves the way for those connected to them.

A groundbreaker's mind-set is different from those around them, and they often pay a great price for change—sometimes even losing their lives or relationships or being ridiculed, ostracized, alienated, and misunderstood. Groundbreakers dare to be different in spite of the possible oppositions. Jesus was a groundbreaker. He freely suffered and died on the cross so that we may be saved. Mary, the mother of Jesus was a groundbreaker, a virgin pregnant with a baby by the Holy Spirit, having not known a man intimately. Can you imagine the talk around the city and the unbelief of the people? Martin Luther King Jr., Rosa Parks, and many others during the civil rights era risked and sometimes lost their lives in the name of freedom and equality; they were groundbreakers.

I want to bring it a little closer to home. As a Christian, the power of one believer can be groundbreaking. The very course of a family can be changed. Generational curses can be broken. Alcoholism, drug abuse, poverty, divorce, hatred, various mind-sets, sexual immorality, and past hurts can be healed. The power of one person, especially those in any leadership role in a company or in a church, can cause change—maybe not on a large scale but one person at a time or one small group at a time, which can then cause a domino effect to people connected to that one person or small group. Although companies and churches are two different entities, they both consist of people. The influences are the same, and one daring to be different can cause positive change.

Being an individual can be challenging and lonely at times; adults can be like a group of children on a playground. Everyone wants to be loved and accepted, but at what cost? It takes courage to be a groundbreaker. Going against the mind-set (a habitual mental attitude that determines how you will interpret and respond to situations) of people is very challenging and hard, but if God said it, things will work out in the end. You may receive some cuts and bruises before it's all over. But that's just the way it is when human beings are involved—and that is why the Lord is who He is.

God will lead you to do things that no one will understand at times—just make sure it is God. Be prayerful and honestly examine your motives to make sure your decision is in God's will. "Trust in the Lord with all thine heart; and lean not unto thine own understanding. In all thine ways acknowledge him, and he shall direct thy paths." (Proverbs 3:5–6 KJV).

Getting married, choosing a career, leaving a job, a marriage, or a church, or making any other life-altering decision is major. "My sheep hear my voice, and I know them, and they follow me" (John 10:27 KJV). Following the voice of the Lord is like walking through a maze, and the only way out is by listening to the voice that is guiding you out. It is a faith walk, trusting and believing in him. Do not make quick decisions because of impatience, impulse, anger, the pressure of a trial, or the grass seeming greener on the other side. Every move you make can affect God's plan for your destiny, career, family, and everyone connected to you—even the onlookers. I have made major decisions in my life and received direction from the Lord through prayer and His Word. They were not always easy and comfortable; in fact, it was just downright scary at times. People didn't always understand and agree with me, but the Lord gave me instructions on how to execute His directions in the most peaceful and godly manner possible. I just obeyed His voice, and each time, I was comforted by His Word.

Painful and cruel circumstances could be part of your growth process; you need to know the difference. I cannot stress enough how important it is to have the Word of God and the Holy Spirit to lead you and guide you into all truth. Patience is a priceless virtue to possess during hard times.

> Knowing that the testing of your faith produces patience. But let patience have *its* perfect work, that you may be perfect and complete, lacking nothing. If any of you lacks wisdom, let him ask of God, who gives to all liberally and without reproach, and it will be given to him. But let him ask in faith, with no doubting, for he who doubts is like

> a wave of the sea driven and tossed by the wind. For let not that man suppose that he will receive anything from the Lord; *he is* a double-minded man, unstable in all his ways. (James 1:3–8 NKJV)

Tests and trials are like lifting weights: the heavier the weights, the greater the results, and the resistance of the weights builds, shapes, and strengthens the spiritual muscles. It does not matter what kind of situation you find yourself in and how difficult things may be, the hand of God is always extended. Take hold, have faith in God's Word, and pray daily. He will see you through your greatest challenge—and He will bless you abundantly!

The Lord will be with you, and He will fight for you if you only trust Him.

> Let us therefore come boldly unto the throne of grace, that we may obtain mercy and find grace to help in time of need. (Hebrews 4:16 NKJV)

God is so awesome. He can do whatever He wants to do—when, however, and to whomever. It amazes me when I hear people say what God will and will not do. He is Lord.

> The Lord is good, a strength *and* stronghold in the day of trouble; He knows [He recognizes, cares for, and understands fully] those who take refuge *and* trust in Him. (Nahum 1:7)

> I will lift up my eyes to the hills—From whence comes my help? My help *comes* from the Lord, Who made heaven and earth. (Psalm 121:1–2 NKJV)

Question: If you are going through something right now, what is your plan of action? What has been one of the most difficult trials in your life? How did you get through it? Are you a stronger person? What did you learn from it?

CHAPTER 4

The Women's Ministry

God's timing is so awesome! Have you ever thought, *Lord, why am I here at this place, at this time?* In our limited knowledge, we cannot see how God will set us in a place and present opportunities to unlock treasures that He has put within us and reveal His purpose for our lives. This is what He did with Joseph and Daniel. Although they were both taken from their homeland, God used the places where they were to bring about His purpose for their lives and others.

The women's ministry at my former church presented opportunities to unlock treasures that God placed within me. I was a participant on a panel of women, providing the opportunity for me to share my past hurts and emotional struggles openly. I told the women about the time I attended a community college when my English instructor asked the class members to write an exit paper about experiences that had caused a turning point in our lives.

I titled my paper "The Agony of Obesity," which turned out to be a confession. My heart burned within me as I wrote it. I told how the desire to eat and the desire to lose weight were equally strong until the inner struggle was impossible to deny. I ate large meals and then took a strong laxative. It became a daily habit, which caused me to be concerned about how I would be endangering my health if I continued.

Once, when placing an order for doughnuts, I purposely said to the salesperson, "Let me see how many *they* want." I was *they,* but I did not want the salesperson to know the entire order was for me. Sadly, I stuffed myself with them all.

In my paper, I also confessed how my weight affected my relationship with a gentleman I was dating at the time. In my heart, I believed my weight was an issue with him. Although he never said anything or treated me in a way that validated my feelings, it was the way I felt about myself. Every time we went out, a commercial would come on the radio that advertised a weight loss program. "I don't want her, you can have her, she's too fat for me, she's too fat for me ..." The song would go on and on, which made me want to sink down into the floor of the car. I glanced at him while the song played, and it appeared as though he did not hear it.

In my paper, I expressed the mixed messages I received from media advertisements and described the time when a billboard on the expressway displayed a woman lying on the beach in a swimsuit: she appeared to be free and not bound by fat. The scene reminded me of a freedom I had never experienced.

On a television commercial advertising a weight loss program, I saw a woman who said, "I'm so glad I joined the weight loss program, and now it's my wedding day!" This told me that if I lost weight, I would get married. During that time, I couldn't stand to look at myself in the mirror.

I summarized my exit paper with details of my Christmas holiday shopping experience at the mall. I tried on many garments that did not fit because I was up to a dress size of 26½. I saw couples walking in the mall, hugging and holding hands, and I thought, *I'll never experience that.* The women seemed so free—free from the worry of how they looked.

I now know some smaller women have the same struggles of not liking themselves either. I got so depressed that I could not take it any longer. I was mentally exhausted and emotionally worn out. I left the mall and headed home. I passed my house, and when the golden arches were in view, I drove up to the drive-through window and heard the familiar greeting, "Welcome to McDonald's! May I help you, please?"

I responded, "Yes, give me a Big Mac, a double cheeseburger, a large order of fries, a chocolate milkshake, a large coke, and an apple pie."

After I paid for the food, I pulled over in the parking lot and started to eat. I tried to eat all the food, but I could not. Looking at myself in the rearview mirror and crying, I said, "Lord, I am out of control. Please help me. I need your help!"

I ended the paper by explaining how exposing my insecurities caused a turning point in my life. It is amazing what prayer can do. Gradually, my thought patterns started changing: "So what? I am overweight. I am somebody, and the whole world is made up of people of different sizes, colors, and shapes. I am going to be the best that I can be." I had to learn to love me. I started focusing on my good points.

When I ended my sharing on the panel, to my surprise, there were many women in the audience who identified with my experience in one way or another. Even though I am still on my weight loss journey, and sometimes my weight goes up and down, God has given me inner peace. I do not get depressed anymore. It is my goal to have victory in this area of my life, but in the meantime, I choose to enjoy the life God has given me!

Looking back, I now know that God ordained for me to be a part of the women's ministry in order to encourage and bless many others. During my fifteen years of speaking in the women's conferences, God gave me topics such as "Help! I'm in an Identity Crisis," "The Hurting Woman," "A Thin Line between Flesh and Spirit," "I Need a Fix," "Inner Hurts," "Self-Inflicted Wounds," and many more. These messages brought emotional healing to me because they were born out my own issues and struggles. Look at God! The hurt and pain I have experienced were used to benefit and heal others as well.

I realize that men have issues too. They feel rejection, they have struggles, and many of the brothers have not had good role models. Men express their pain differently than women, and like never before, they are participating in men's conferences all over the world, seeking direction and guidance. They are learning to be real with themselves by expressing their feelings and confessing their inner struggles. They are seeking God now more than ever because they have a great responsibility as men. God ordained it to be so, and what better way is there for this to be accomplished than by going after the One who made them? I believe there is a special anointing when we can be vulnerable and confess our struggles at an appropriate time as God permits.

We are all in a battle, and many die in the middle of it—but you do not have to. Turning your eyes toward the Lord Jesus Christ and His Word is the first step to freedom.

CHAPTER 5

Jesus, Solid Like a Rock

I love the scripture "I will love thee, O Lord, my strength. The Lord is my rock, and my fortress, and my deliverer; my God, my strength, in whom I will trust; my buckler, and the horn of my salvation, and my high tower." (Psalms 18:1-2 KJV) After many years of searching for love, approval, acceptance, validation, appreciation, and affirmation, I now know that I was searching for it in all the wrong places.

I suffered with depression for most of my young life and into adulthood. I cried a lot, and I felt my life was not worth living. At times, I wondered why I was created and what my purpose was in life. On several occasions, I would get a hotel room to be alone and sort my feelings. Since I did not know what my feelings were, all I did was cry.

Once I sought help at the neighborhood mental health center. I noticed the counselor I was seeing that day was pregnant. From my personal perception, not knowing if she was single or married, I felt that she had more problems than I did, which is why I did not keep my next appointment.

Socially, I appeared to have it all together. In fact, I was the life of the party, but when I arrived home, I cried myself to sleep. I cannot remember anything that was going on in my mind; all I knew was that life did not feel good to me. Every day, I fought voices that told me to kill myself. I literally spoke back to those voices and said, "I will not kill myself. I am going to give my heart to Jesus one day." I truly believed that it would happen one day, but I did not know when. I enjoyed living a sinful life until I began to realize that my relationships, the marijuana, and the partying were not satisfying the hunger and longing I felt in my soul.

I wanted more in life; I needed a change. I started doing what my mother taught my sisters and me to do as children: pray. Instead of just crying after leaving the crowd, I started asking the Lord to come into my life and change me. I knew my mother and other family members were concerned and praying for me.

My mother would gather her four little girls in her bedroom on bended knees and pray. Since I was the oldest, I had to lead the prayer first. My other sisters would follow, and my mother would be last. So many times, we saw her weeping before the Lord for herself and for us.

Hallelujah! I am so glad my mother prayed for me. I thank God for the mother I had. She used so much wisdom when dealing with me. She never called me crazy, and she did not put me down. I already felt down and crazy, but my mother prayed and loved me in spite of myself.

The holidays were depressing because the devil would torment me with thoughts of how I looked. He tormented me with lies about what my relatives were going say to me during the family gatherings, such as "You've gotten so fat" or "You're so big." However, they never spoke negatively to me about my weight. I only received unconditional love, and I was greeted with hugs and kisses. I felt total acceptance from them.

Although I asked the Lord to come into my life and change me, I told Him that I did not know how He was going to do it. I recounted to Him all the things I was taught as a child: what a Christian does not do and how I would not be able to stop doing them if I accepted Him into my life. Giving up partying, smoking cigarettes, marijuana, and sex seemed like a lot of ungodly habits to overcome.

He spoke to me one day during one of my conversations with Him in a way that I could understand. He said, "How can you knock something you've never tried?"

I responded, "Okay, I'm going to trust you."

On a Saturday evening shortly after that conversation, I told my boyfriend that I was going to give my life to the Lord on that Sunday. Not knowing it yet, I smoked my last joint that night and smoked my last cigarette on the way to church. As I entered the church doors and took my seat, I did not know what to expect. I said within my heart, "Okay, Lord, here I am."

As far as I could tell, there was nothing special that happened. I did not feel any chills, and I was not called to the altar or given a personal word by the pastor. After the service, not knowing that God had done an awesome thing in me, an opportunity was presented to smoke some marijuana, which I had never declined before.

I said, "No!" Something strange was going on within me. I left that place and never returned.

While driving home, I noticed people smoking in their cars and on the street corners. The thought ran through my mind that I had been destroying my body. I realized that I had been blind in sin for a long time.

When I arrived at my apartment, I packed up all the ashtrays and went to my stash where all the roaches (the ends from marijuana cigarettes) were kept from the last two lids of marijuana I had bought, and I flushed them down the commode. Look at the power of God: a change had come over me!

On my way to work the next morning, I noticed that a two-week tent revival was starting at a church in my neighborhood. I decided to attend the meeting after work, and I asked my aunt to attend the meeting with me.

As we entered the tent, I went to the front row, and she took a seat in the back. I was hungry for the Word of God and ready for a continual change in my life.

The preacher shouted about how you must be born again, come out of sin, and stop committing adultery and fornication. Stop your lying, give up hatred and strife, and put down the cigarettes. I thought, *What else must I do?* I was willing to do whatever the preacher said. Praise God!

After that two-week revival, I was a new creature. I joined the church that hosted the revival.

> Therefore if any man be in Christ, he is a new creature: old things are passed away; behold, all things are become new. (2 Corinthians 5:17 KJV)

Even though I was free from depression, I still had to periodically fight those old, familiar feelings of sadness and despair. I was determined to hold on to my salvation. When those feelings came to visit, listening to gospel music, thinking on the goodness of Jesus, giving thanks, and—most of all—reading the Word of God made them flee. During those times, I learned not to serve God by my feelings because our feelings will deceive us. What's important is to keep doing what is right, staying in the Word of God and in prayer. This journey we are on is by faith, not by feelings.

If you deal with depression, you must fight with the Word of God in faith to stay free.

> Submit yourselves therefore to God. Resist the devil, and he will flee from you. (James 4:7 KJV)

Be knowledgeable of the people and the things that cause you to fall into depression. You have a choice to succumb to those feelings or not. Be aware of the feelings of hopelessness and the feelings of never measuring up. Watch out for the doom-and-gloom feelings since they are traps of depression.

> For we walk by faith, not by sight. (2 Corinthians 5:7 KJV)

> Finally, brethren, whatsoever things are true, whatsoever things are honest, whatsoever things are just, whatsoever things are pure, whatsoever things are lovely, whatsoever things are of good report; if there be any virtue, and if there be any praise, think on these things. (Philippians 4:8 KJV)

Renewing your mind in the Word of God can make a world of difference in your life. Some people suffer with depression due to medical conditions. God is not against you seeking the help of medical professionals and seeking godly spiritual counsel. I have found that focusing on Jesus Christ will keep your mind stable. Depending on Him will keep you settled in your spirit. Jesus Christ is a firm foundation. He is solid like a rock.

David often expressed his dependence on the Lord:

> I will love thee, O Lord, my strength. The Lord is my rock, and my fortress, and my deliverer; my God, my strength, in whom I will trust; my buckler, and the horn of my salvation, and my high tower. (Psalm 18:1–2 KJV)

> The LORD is my light and my salvation; whom shall I fear? (Psalm 27:1 KJV)

Keeping my eyes upon the Lord gives me unspeakable joy because there is no one like Him. Words cannot express the comfort and the freedom I feel knowing that I have Jesus in my life and by my side, knowing He will fight every battle. He knows my every intention, and He is everything I need, which does not mean that I do not need people. Jesus is my "personal Savior" and holds a special place in my heart. I cannot put people in the spot where the Lord is. He does not have the same tendencies as humankind.

> "For My thoughts *are* not your thoughts, Nor *are* your ways My ways," says the Lord. "For

> *as* the heavens are higher than the earth, So are My ways higher than your ways, And My thoughts than your thoughts." (Isaiah 55:8–9 NKJV)

Each waiting moment I have experienced with the Lord is an opportunity for me to know Him even more.

Humankind has the tendency to love you today and hate you tomorrow; speak well and evil of you with the same breath. That is a part of human behavior.

God allows disappointments regardless of whom they come through, and He will allow us to disappoint others so that none of us will lose focus on who He is. The next time someone hurts you or disappoints you, forgive them because not all of us are on the same spiritual level. We have different strengths and weaknesses; we all come from different walks in life and have different experiences. Forgiveness, however, is universal, and we all need it.

I have been through the stage of blaming people for what they did or did not do; it is the they-should-have or they-could-have stage. I fight to stay free from all that now. Turning my eyes toward the Lord takes my focus off people's inclinations, faults, and frailties.

> The fear of man brings a snare, But whoever trusts in *and* puts his confidence in the Lord will be exalted *and* safe. (Proverbs 29:25)

There is always safety when we put our confidence in the Lord.

CHAPTER 6

A Little Girl's Thirst

My dad was an entrepreneur and a very hard worker all his life. My mom always supported him in all his business endeavors. Together, they owned several businesses at various times.

When I was a child, my parents owned a childcare center, called the Williams' Kiddie Ranch, a trucking service that hauled dirt to construction sites, a mail carrier service with the Post Office that collected mail from surrounding rural areas, a barbecue rib shack, and—my favorite—a grocery store and neighborhood café. I honestly do not see how they made a profit after my three sisters and I enjoyed unlimited trips to the chips, candy, and cookie counters. Looking back, it amazes me they never said, "Stop! You're eating up our profits!"

We always had a roof over our heads, plenty of food to eat, and nice clothes to wear. We attended a private school one year and had a nanny who assisted my mom while she helped manage the business. After my parents divorced, my dad continued to seek new business opportunities and relocated to Tampa, Florida, where he owned the Williams' One-Stop Groceries. He sold live crabs, barbecue—his specialty—and his own pork skins called Williams' Skins.

Although my dad was very responsive to our physical needs, as a little girl, I yearned to hear him say, "I love you!" I felt an emptiness within, and I craved his approval. I did whatever he asked me to do. For example, one time, I helped him with bleeding the brakes on his dump truck, which was a hard task.

He would say, "Push! Push!" But after the task was completed, he never said a word.

I wondered if the job I did was good enough, but my thoughts remained with me. Many times, I asked myself, "What could I do to gain his approval?" I needed to hear some words of affirmation, but they never came.

Maybe he just did not know what I needed. On one occasion, I brought home a bad report card. He was very upset with me because he felt I could do better. That night, while doing my homework, I remember him pushing my head down continually into my study book and saying, "Study! Study!" His reaction made me feel that I could not do anything right. His correction was always associated with a strong tone and a stern, displeasing facial expression. There were times when the sound of his truck coming up the driveway compelled me to get up and appear busy. It was like walking on eggshells when he was around.

My dad also had a humorous side. He had a way of making us laugh when he stood outside our bedroom window and yelled, "Wee, wee, wee, wee," trying to scare us! He could say some of the funniest things that would have us busting at the seams, and I enjoyed hearing him laugh.

My mom was a cheerful, loving, and nurturing mother who made great efforts to please my dad. On one occasion, we had been out all day, and dinner was not ready when he came home, which was rare. He asked my mom for the reason. She started explaining where we had been, and she said we went this place and that place, adding, "Isn't that right, girls?"

We said, "Yes, ma'am."

He said, "I'm tired of your 'Yes, ma'am,' girls." He took a wet dishcloth and attempted to slap all four of us on our faces, going down the line, but I ducked before he got to me.

One morning after my daddy dropped us off at school, I remember crying in the restroom because of something that had happened at home and being comforted by a classmate. It is amazing how children can be affected by an unhealthy situation in the home. I witnessed my mom enduring a lot from my dad, including infidelity.

She finally got the courage to divorce him, and I was glad for many reasons. For one, the new atmosphere in the home was wonderful, although that was when we experienced the financial struggles of a single-parent household. Looking back on things as an adult, I often wondered why she was passive and took so much from him. I believe she also longed for my dad's love and approval. He knew he had a good wife, but he took her for granted. Years later, when we were adults, my mom remarried to a longtime friend. My dad continued to live in our community, and my mom always said, "He is still your dad, so you should love and respect him."

One day, my dad came by the house with a young man and said, "I want you to meet your brother."

Imagine how shocked we were to find out we had a brother who was older than us! I was not sure if my mom knew about him. However, we welcomed him into our lives with open arms. There was no denying that he was our brother because he resembled my dad and my sisters.

My brother eventually came to live with us. Years later, I asked him why he made that decision.

He responded, "Well, Dad and I had a disagreement. To my understanding, we had a bachelor pad, and I had a female guest in my bedroom. Suddenly Dad burst through the door and said, 'There is only one player in the house, and that is me.' I got angry, and your mom kindly allowed me to move in with you all."

We shook our heads and said, "That's our daddy!"

I was the only sibling who worked with my dad at Williams' Barbecue Rib Shack. I thought, *See, Dad? I'm working hard for you.* It was the cry of my heart. I was endlessly seeking affirmations from him.

Questions: Can you identify with these desires from your childhood? Did you hunger for love, approval, and validation? As an adult, you may still have the same hunger from your mother, father, husband, wife, the person you are dating, children, church family, spiritual leaders, and employers.

When I was in twelfth grade, my dad would see me driving an unfamiliar car in our community from time to time. Instead of him questioning me about whose car I was driving, he assumed the car belonged to some older man who had allowed me to drive his car for sexual favors. Unfortunately, his suspicion may have come from something he had done before, which was to use women.

While I was at my boyfriend's apartment with some other friends, my mom called to tell me that my daddy was parked in the driveway. I asked my boyfriend to let me drive his car home and told him I would be back. As I drove up the driveway, I could see my dad's car parked with the lights out. He was sitting, waiting, stewing, and allowing his mind to run wild.

After I parked the car, as my dad approached me, I rolled down the window and said, "Hey, Daddy!"

He immediately slapped me hard until my face went numb. He later realized that I was a young woman who was almost out of high school, I was ready to attend technical school, and the car belonged to my boyfriend who was not an "old man." I never heard him apologize for his harsh treatment. Talk about a misuse of authority!

I have heard that my mom dated a man named Ike (not Tina Turner's Ike) prior to my dad coming along and sweeping her off her feet. I wondered if Ike was my real dad because I looked different from my sisters. I was overweight, and my skin complexion was lighter. The man I called "Daddy" just could not be my dad. Maybe Ike was a different type of man. Maybe he was someone I could respect and enjoy being around, not fearing and being relieved when I was away from him. Maybe I could experience a real father-daughter relationship with him. I spent time on many occasions secretly searching the house for proof that I was adopted or that I was Ike's child. I never asked my mom if my suspicions were true; I just kept them in my heart.

After my mom died during my early twenties, I got the courage to ask one of my aunts if what I pondered all those years were true. She confirmed that Ike was not my dad. Right then, those thoughts faded away.

In my later years, while working as a director of a childcare center, I saw many fathers bringing and picking up their children, and some were more noticeable than others. Whenever I had the chance, I encouraged the fathers by letting them know just how important they were to their children and that the impact of their presence in their children's lives was priceless and ordained by God. When I saw a little girl leave the building in her father's arms, I said to myself, "Wow!" I wondered how that felt, thinking she was so blessed! On the other hand, I saw how children were devastated when their parents argued, fought, or separated. Whatever your experiences were as a child, Jesus can heal and fill the void. "When my father and my mother forsake me, then the Lord will take me up" (Psalm 27:10 KJV).

I told the Lord, "If you were like man, I don't know what I would do." I am so glad I can approach the Lord without fear. I know Him and have experienced His constant love, patience and, grace—even in times of correction. I believe the Lord allows things to happen in our lives to show us the supernatural love and grace that sets Him apart from humankind.

Question: Even though you know the Word of God, what is your perception of God toward you? Do you believe God loves you unconditionally even when you mess up?

During one of my prayer times, I had the most wonderful experience with the Lord. I was praying for God to heal me from layers of inner fears and hurts when a vision of my mom and dad appeared before me. They were waving and smiling, and the Spirit of the Lord revealed to me to wave back.

I thought, *Wave back?*

He said, "Wave back and say bye to what they did and did not do. Forgive them and let it all go."

I began to wave back, crying. I literally said bye while forgiving them. It was revealed to me that my dad was doing what he thought was right by providing a roof over our heads and feeding and clothing us. He knew nothing about nurturing, but he did know about making money. In his mind, he was being a good dad. Perhaps he was treating me the way his parents had treated him.

Parents were different in the forties and fifties; unless we learn a better way of doing things, we remain ignorant, continuing in our familiar ways. My mom was only being the way she knew how to be: an old-school mom and a submissive wife. She wanted her marriage to work, and that was why she endured a lot from my dad. She was mimicking the example of my grandmother.

After prayer, and from that time on, I never felt or referred to myself as a victim of my childhood hurts and fears where my mom and dad were concerned. I was set free!

Do not place God in a box, thinking you know how, when, where, or through whom your deliverance will come. He will use whatever means necessary to deliver you if you are serious about being free. Just trust God, have patience, and take it one day at a time. Continue to pray in faith and enjoy your journey.

Casting all your cares [all your anxieties, all your worries, and all your concerns, once and for all] on Him, for He cares about you [with deepest affection, and watches over you very carefully]. (1 Peter 5:7).

He healeth the broken in heart, and bindeth up their wounds. (Psalm 147:3 KJV)

CHAPTER 7

Grown Woman, Little Girl

It is my wedding day, November 16, at six o'clock. The church is full, and the program is going as planned. The preacher, the groom, and the best man are all at the altar. The guests stand because it is time for my grand entrance.

The door opens, and all eyes are on me. The room is filled with joy and excitement. I can hear the comments: "She's so beautiful" and "You're so pretty." I can see the smiles on the people's faces, and I have full view of the altar.

The soloist is singing.

Nobody knows, including the bride herself, that they were watching a grown woman with little-girl issues walking down the aisle to be joined to a man with his own set of little-boy issues.

Life has a way of bringing our unknown personal issues to the surface, using our jobs, singleness, finances, marriages, relationships, and even our churches. Until we have been tested and tried in the fire—that's right, the fire—our issues may never surface. The fire will burn away all impurities. If you can endure the process, you will come out as pure gold. *Enduring* is the issue.

After being a single Christian woman for many years, a close friend introduced me to my future husband. We talked several times over the phone before we met. A year later, I invited him along with my friend and her husband for a candlelight dinner. What I loved most about him was that he treated me like fine gold and accepted me just the way I was—weight and all.

During our courtship, we visited each other's churches before he asked me to marry him. I knew it was a big step, and I earnestly sought the Lord with fasting and prayer for direction before saying yes. Although we were both Christians, I told the Lord that I would not marry him if it was not His will. I realized that marriage—as God designed it—takes love, patience, and commitment to endure the process of two people with their own set of expectations and personal issues becoming one.

Unknowingly, sometimes the root cause of our troubles stems from unresolved childhood issues.

The first years of our marriage were difficult for me because of my expectations. Unsuccessfully, I spent a lot of time trying to get him be the way I had always dreamed a Christian husband would be. I wanted him to talk kinder and gentler, but unconsciously, he spoke with a harsh tone and was quick and to the point. I had a deep and inward thirst for kind words, which I thought would make me feel special—a desire of both men and women.

I thank God for a dear friend at my church who often encouraged me. In my times of frustration, we had many long phone conversations. I remember calling and asking her to meet me in the Walmart parking lot. Her wise and godly counsel helped me through the tough times.

After leaving our long, woman-to-woman talks, I would have a new attitude! I went home and prepared my husband something he loved—a big breakfast for dinner with homemade biscuits, which took a lot of effort. Although, I could have bought frozen or canned biscuits, I put my heart and soul into making them from scratch because, for me, the blessing was in the extra effort it took to make them. I developed an attitude that whatever I did for my husband, I did it as unto the Lord.

> Whatever you do [whatever your task may be], work from the soul [that is, put in your very best effort], as [something done] for the Lord and not for men. (Colossians 3:23).

I call it sowing and planting. I changed my focus from my husband to the Word of God.

Finally, I decided to accept my husband for who he was. I decided to love him and pray for him—and let God do the rest. After all, we both had issues, and in the meantime, I decided to work on my self-worth, self-esteem, and loving myself in a healthy way. I began to draw from the well that never runs dry—Jesus.

It became obvious to me that emotionally I felt like a little girl in a grown woman's body, and I did not know it until I got married. I had many layers of issues that God had to help me with. Outwardly, I appeared strong, but inwardly, I was timid and easily controlled and manipulated out of a fear of not being loved.

When it came to close, intimate relationships, I was unfamiliar with setting healthy boundaries because I did not see it demonstrated as a child between my mother and father. However, as I prayed about my desires, the Lord revealed to me that I had the same hunger for compliments and affirmations that I had as a little girl because I did not receive them from my dad.

The Lord enlightened my understanding that I have value and encouraged me to look within to see my own self-worth. That knowledge brought freedom to me. I started on a new journey and began to enjoy and appreciate my life on a different level. I took the power away from people to control how I felt about myself. Instead of waiting for my husband to compliment and affirm me, I began to look in the mirror and see my own beauty. I would say to myself, "Girl, you look good!" My inward thirst was quenched, and my life was made better. Through this experience, I am much stronger and more fulfilled. I now receive compliments and affirmation from my husband, but I do not crave them.

As my journey continued, I asked my husband to take me to the movies, but he wanted to work on his car. The Lord gently impressed on me how to enjoy life myself by taking myself to the movies—something I had never thought to do before. I said to myself, *Yes, I can do this!* I got dressed and told my husband, without an attitude on my part, where I was going. I chose to see a funny movie, bought some popcorn, and enjoyed my own company.

I had a blast and laughed throughout the entire movie. What a freedom I experienced that evening.

On another occasion, the Lord taught me how to take care of myself. I asked my husband to bring me a glass of water. He did what I requested, but he brought me a glass of lukewarm water from the kitchen faucet. I thanked him for it.

The Lord gently asked, "Do you want lukewarm water or ice-cold water?"

I said, "I want ice-cold water."

He said, "Get up and get it yourself."

I got up peacefully and got it myself. Later, I had the opportunity to share the incident with my husband, and from that time on, if I asked for water, he made sure it was ice water. Sometimes we may desire things from people who are not capable or not willing to give us. How wonderful and marvelous it is to know that what people cannot give, do not know how to give, or will not give, God will give.

At church my husband and I learned about setting healthy boundaries and so much more. Our marriage benefited as our former pastor and first lady poured themselves into the congregation. They constantly shared the many faults, struggles, and difficulties they endured in their marriage, especially in the beginning years. Through the Word of God, they taught about forgiveness, letting go of past hurts, and the danger of holding on to those hurts. That was when I learned to take a stand as a wife appropriately. They taught us balance in confronting issues, which offered hope in seeing how God had moved in their lives.

Through faith, obedience, prayer, and patience, we were able to release the baggage we both had brought into our marriage. The Lord is continuing to do His work in us. Regardless of your past or present issues, there is healing and deliverance in Jesus. The Lord has a way of showing us ourselves. The Word of God is like a mirror and is as powerful as a hammer. It knocks and pulls down anything that is not like God, and it builds and shapes us into new creatures.

> For the Word of God is quick, and powerful, and sharper than any two-edged sword, piercing even to the dividing asunder of the soul and spirit, and of the joints and marrow, and is a discerner of the thoughts and intents of the heart. (Hebrews 4:12 KJV)

Questions: What past or present issues are you continually dealing with? What generational traits and sins are affecting your life? Is it anger, bitterness, hatred, violence, drugs, prostitution, adultery, fornication, children born out of wedlock or incest, pornography, or unnatural affections?

Regardless of how badly you want someone to change, that person must first see the need for change and then want to change. The ways of some people are unhealthy and deeply rooted. If you are trying to change someone, beware that you can get worn out in the process. Focus on yourself and pray for the person. There is always a lesson to learn in any situation. I prayed many times, "Lord, raise me above any unhealthy circumstance. Lord, give me hinds' feet because I refuse to be trampled on and crushed.

> He makes my feet like hinds' feet [able to stand firmly and tread safely on paths of testing and trouble]; He sets me [securely] upon my high places. (Psalm 18:33)

Lord, make me wise as a serpent and humble as a dove. Show me how to handle this person or situation, in Jesus's name. There is power in prayer and in the name of Jesus. Leaning on the Lord in tough situations is all we have. If anything is going to be done, let the Lord do it. Let it begin with you.

CHAPTER 8

Don't Run from the Process

I would like to make one thing clear right now: because we live in this present world, we will always have something to deal with. These words may seem a little harsh, but I cannot stress it enough. Wanting to escape life and everything that comes with it is not healthy thinking. I used to look at my baby picture, pacing the floor and crying because I wanted to go back to being a baby. I did not like life because it was almost too difficult for me to handle. Looking at my baby picture reminded me of a time of not having to deal with anything. I know it sounds strange, but that was the way I thought and felt in the past. As I look at it now, it was all a part of my process. Thank God, I made it through.

The devil had a plan to destroy me and keep me from my destiny, but God also had a plan. His plan was to give me life through salvation, to get the glory from my life, to heal every hurt, to give me liberty, to set me free because I was bound, to comfort me, to give me beauty for ashes, and to give me the oil of joy and the garment of praise for the spirit of heaviness (paraphrase of Isaiah 61:1–3.)

Living life is a process because we are faced with many things, but how we handle our process determines our outcome. Enduring our personal process has its rewards if we go through the struggles with an open heart to grow. Consider all you have been through, all you are experiencing now, and all you will face in the future as not just for you but for someone else. The knowledge learned and the wisdom gained are priceless.

The inner strength you develop from your personal process is awesome and will be used for the glory of God. He wants to use you, but you must go through and endure your process. The words previously stated—*awesome, inner strength, wisdom, knowledge,* and *the glory of God*—sound good, but the process does not come easy and it comes with a price.

There were times when it felt like the Lord was not with me, but He was. Just think about it: if I had followed the devil's suggestion to commit suicide, this book would not have been written today. Even though I had to face many things—some good, some bad, some bitter, and some sweet—some of it was before knowing Jesus Christ, and a lot of it was after knowing Him.

If my mother had given up and stopped praying and loving me—in words and in deeds—I would not be here today. I know she was concerned and worried many nights when I stayed out late, but I had a course to run, my personal course. I thought I was doing something, not knowing that when I was not at home by a certain time, Mama would get my sisters up and say, "Girls, get up. Let's pray. Valeria is not home." Prayer kept me safe and brought me home.

Before my mother died, she saw her prayers answered: I accepted Christ into my life. I am still on the battlefield of life, and I am not tired yet. If parents pray, seek God for wisdom and guidance, and let Him have their troubled, hardheaded, and rebellious children, the rewards will be great. Sometimes parents act out of their frustrations and emotions, which can get in God's way and make the process worse. Fixing these things is more easily said than done.

Because of the perilous times we are living in, even our loved ones may choose destructive and dangerous paths for themselves, which can also impact the safety and well-being of the family. In this case, ask God to cover you all with His blood and seek wise counsel (legal and spiritual). Whatever your process is, do not run from it.

It may be ugly, painful, unpleasant, or uncomfortable right now, but remain determined. Lean hard on the Lord, have faith, and trust in Him, and He will see you through. Do not run from the challenges and the trials you may be encountering because they are a part of the journey God has for you. Your family members, spouse, friends, associates, your place of worship, and even your enemies are a part of God's plan. Taking a new job or losing your current one, starting new relationships, getting married and having children, being single, and dealing with life and death are all part of the process. Do not run; go through it.

You may be experiencing many types of fears: fear of failure or success, of moving out of your comfort zone, of not being loved, of loneliness or rejection, of making mistakes or being made ashamed, of getting hurt or hurting others, of failing God, of being overlooked, or of not measuring up to people's standards and expectations.

Maybe you have a fear of divorce or abandonment and fear that God will not answer your prayers. This list can go on and on. I have heard it said that the acronym for *fear* is merely *false evidence appearing real.*

Question: What are you afraid of? Pause and take time to search inside yourself. Admit your fears to the Lord and ask Him to forgive and help you. Make positive confessions daily until they get in your spirit, such as: the Lord shall supply all my needs according to his riches in glory by Christ Jesus; I walk by faith and not by sight; the Lord has not given me the spirit of fear but of power and of love and a sound mind; I am encouraged, and my heart is strengthened because my hope is in the Lord; I will walk in peace; I am blessed, and my family is blessed and will live according to God's Holy Word; and I am forgiven. You can make your own list based on truths from the Bible.

I confronted my fear and asked myself, Can I write a book—even though the challenge is bigger than I am? I chose to do it afraid because "I can do all things through Christ who strengthens me" (Philippians 4:19 NKJV). Praise God!

CHAPTER 9

Blindsided by Inner Hurts

I define inner hurts as internal wounds or internal scars. They give the sensation or the feeling of pain. From my experience and perspective, they can damage us or deform our growth emotionally, mentally, physically, verbally, and socially. Abuse of various kinds—rejection, sexual abuse, abandonment, and neglect—cause physical pain and inner pain. An unhealthy environment that consists of uncontrolled anger, violence, harshness or strictness, alcoholism, drugs, and sexual perverseness can also cause inner hurts.

Hurts can devastate, handicap, paralyze, and cripple us. They can cause deep-seated anger, low self-esteem, and unhealthy fears. In addition to the fears previously mentioned, unhealthy fears can also include a fear of authority figures (parents, older siblings, teachers, bosses, police, etc.), a fear of religious authority figures (pastors, bishops, apostles, etc.), and a fear of losing control in life situations (job, house, car, husband, children, etc.). These fears can cause us to develop stress and anxiety attacks, which sometimes give a false sense of having a heart attack or even the feeling like you are losing your mind.

Inner hurts can be displayed in many ways, such as seeking validation; developing a feeling of numbness; experiencing false guilt; or having a personality that is overbearing, controlling, dominating, or bullying, which can affect your relationships with your parents, your young children, and even your adult children, husband, wife, family, friends, coworkers, or church family. If left unchecked or unaccountable, your family, business, and church will suffer bitterness, low morale, unproductivity, and the loss of good people. Signs of inner hurts are unhealthy boundary issues that prevent you from saying no. Other signs of inner hurts are being too timid or having a warped perception (thinking and reasoning); displaying obsessive behavior in eating or cleaning, overworking, overachieving; or not wanting to face the past or the future. We sometimes make inner vows that develop attitudes and wrong thought systems.

Inner hurts will blind you from your real issue. In other words, hurts will sometimes blind you from yourself—even if it is obvious to others that you are a hurting person. They will mislead you and cause you to put the blame on other people, keep you from having healthy perceptions, and cause you to refuse to deal with issues in a healthy manner.

Inner hurts can cause you to run from man to man, woman to woman, job to job, or church to church—never settling down or committing to anything. Unresolved inner hurts develop into unhealthy behavior patterns that might cause parents to destroy their own family, a husband or wife to destroy their marriage, or someone to chase good people out of their life, cheating them all out of healthy relationships. Even inner hurts will cause a pastor to destroy their own ministry. Unresolved inner hurts create strongholds that will hold you captive and keep you from knowing God's will for your life.

I was almost blindsided by my many layers of inner hurts, but the Lord did not allow them to surface all at once. Various situations will arise in our lives that will awaken issues that have laid dormant within us for years. Despite the pain we feel on the inside, this is really God's way of bringing our attention to an area within us where we need to be made whole. That is what happened to me, when after twelve years of being a Christian, I had to come face-to-face with a childhood issue. At first, men with strong personalities brought to the surface many hurts and fears that had laid dormant within me. I started experiencing the feeling of powerlessness, fear of displeasing, and fear of the misuse of authority. There was no escaping those emotions. It was like a head-on collision with destiny: I was being squeezed and pressed all at once but from various areas in my life. I finally had to deal with the root of my problem, which stemmed back to my childhood. However, as I continued to search deep within for the root of these issues, I remembered they were also present during my elementary school days when interacting with my classmates who had strong personalities in the form of bullying. I felt as if I had no voice to stop them from running over me. I was timid and did not know how to stand up for myself.

As a young girl in our home, my feelings were suppressed, and they did not seem to be valid or valuable. I thought, *Is it right for me to question my daddy's behavior or acknowledge that he was wrong for the way he ruled our home with his harsh tones and unpleasant facial expressions? As child what was I to do? Should I have ignored his behavior and just dealt with it because that's the way it is with authority figures?* These questions may seem very naïve, but I was a child and naïve. Because of these encounters, as an adult, the fear of people with strong personalities in authority became a stronghold in my life.

I prayed for the Lord to free me and mature me on the inside. I asked the Lord for wisdom, knowledge, understanding, clarity, and balance in my reasoning and thinking. I was tired of feeling emotionally unhealthy. I needed someone to confide in who would hear me with her heart and not just with her ears.

When we are expressing our feelings, they can sound ugly at times, and talking to the wrong person can do more harm than good. However, God heard my cry. He allowed an evangelist in our church to take the time to talk with me without judging. I knew my thoughts and understanding were distorted and warped because of my experiences. After the crying and sobbing, the evangelist prayed with me, and because of that, I would never forget what she did for me. Even though she did not have all the answers, just being free to express my feelings in a safe environment started me on the road to inner healing. I never heard her speak of our conversation again.

I am a witness that if you pray, God will send someone you can connect with—a person who will be a blessing to your soul. Because the root of my issues had run so deep and for so long in my life, I could not see how God was going to free me.

I cannot say when I was set free, but I know how—it was the power of the Spirit of God that destroyed the chain that bound me. Please hear me: whatever your issue is, with prayer, faith in His Word, and patience, the Lord will deliver you! I weathered the temptation to run from my home, my job, and my church, but by staying, I got the victory.

Blindsided means to attack (someone) from an unseen or unexpected direction.[1] Inner hurts can come from many unexpected and surprising areas in our lives, but we need to know how to handle the hurts and know what to do when an attack comes.

> It is good for me that I have been afflicted; that I might learn thy statutes. (Psalm 119:71 KJV)

Looking back over my life at the difficulties I have faced through people's shortcomings or flaws, *which we all have,* caused me to run to the Lord for wisdom,

---

[1] Merriam-Webster, "Blindsided," https://www.merriam-webster.com/dictionary/blindsided, accessed February 25, 2018.

comfort, guidance, understanding, and healing, which enriched my life greatly. Every person, every pain, and every experience became a vital part of my destiny.

Questions: Do you repeatedly experience the same things, even though they may come from different people and different situations? Is it possible that your recurring situations may be stemming from issues within you? Because hurts can cloud our judgment, blind us from ourselves, and cause us to point the finger, is someone else always to blame? The Lord is not always revealing other people's bad points, but He will show us our own faults when necessary. I love the hymn that says, "It's me, it's me, it's me, O Lord, standing in the need of prayer; not my brother, not my sister, but it's me, O Lord, standing in the need of prayer."

Could it be that you have some unresolved hurts from your past, blindsiding you from the real problem? I know the answers to these questions may be hard to accept, but only when you face the truth about yourself can you be made free. Stop the chaos that is connected to unresolved inner hurts in your life! We only live once. Do not allow circumstances to hinder you from enjoying your life—the abundant life—that God has ordained for you. Your past hurts and ugly circumstances, if you continue to allow them to, will hinder you from knowing true freedom and joy. Take the opportunity today to grow and experience His forgiveness, His power, and His transforming love beyond your inner hurts.

Jesus wants us to know Him in such an awesome way. He wants us to seek to know Him and His love more than any human being because He is true love and everlasting. We can trust Him because He is all-knowing, and He is all wisdom. It is through Him that our needs are met. He knows what we have need of before we ask. He wants to live in and use us for His glory. Most of all, He wants His love to radiate from us to the whole world, which cannot be done if we are bound.

Turn your heart toward Him today and seek Him through prayer and His Word as never before.

> Come unto me, all ye that labour and are heavy laden, and I will give you rest. Take my yoke upon you, and learn of me; for I am meek and lowly in heart: and ye shall find rest unto your souls. For my yoke is easy, and my burden is light. (Matthew 11:28–30 KJV)

ABOUT THE AUTHOR

Valeria W. Stubbs, a native of Atlanta, Georgia, has served faithfully more than thirty-one years in many areas of ministry, ranging from Sunday school teacher (youth and adult), Sunday school superintendent, music department (choir and praise team), drama department director, driver for van ministry, youth department team member, and ministerial staff member. She has worked closely with her pastor's wife as an annual women's conference speaker for more than ten years, and at various times, she has headed the pastoral appreciation committee. Valeria has a God-given passion and listening ear for hurting people, and she is a mentor and friend to many. In 2009, she was called to work beside her husband (Pastor Richard Stubbs) in ministry as first lady of Walking by Faith Christian Ministries in Griffin, Georgia.

Valeria shares with her readers the behind-the-scenes and the under-the-surface strongholds that she experienced. In *Who Will Love Me?* she reveals the insights that God gave her on the strategies of the devil to keep us in bondage through inner hurts. She shares her times of disappointments and her longing to be loved by people who were not capable of filling her emptiness, which only God can fill.

This insightful book will be helpful for many to grow and develop spiritually, socially, and psychologically.

> The Lord God is my strength [my source of courage, my invincible army]; He has made my feet [steady and sure] like hinds' feet. And makes me walk [forward with spiritual confidence] on my high places [of challenge and responsibility]. (Habakkuk 3:19)

ACKNOWLEDGMENTS

I want to acknowledge my Savior and Friend, the Lord Jesus Christ, who inspired me to write this book, a task that was bigger than I could have ever conceived of. All the glory belongs to God. He means everything to me. I cannot imagine life without Him.

To my husband, Richard, thank you, darling, for your full support. If it were not for you, I would not be who I am today. Thank you for allowing me the time to write this book. We both have grown and matured through the years, and marrying you is one of my greatest decisions I have made in life.

To Walking by Faith Christian Ministries thank you for your enthusiasm and support.

To Elder Lachion Morgan, my sister, friend, supporter, and armor barrier for many years, thank you for your valuable input, dedication, and commitment to aid in the editing of this book as a part of the *Who Will Love Me?* Team. Your patience and many talents have been a blessing to me.

To Dr. H. L Morgan, pastor and founder of Tabernacle of Joy Miracle Deliverance Center, Inc., thank you for your book *Bitterness: A Destroyer of Destiny,* which is a great inspiration to many. Your preaching and teaching thrusted me into my destiny. To Co-Pastor V. B. Morgan, of Tabernacle of Joy Miracle Deliverance Center, Inc., Tabernacle is blessed because of you. Thank you for the opportunity to work with you in the women's ministry for many years. You are an awesome example to many women and first ladies.

To Bishop Thomas, pastor, and Dr. Bobbie Daniels, co-pastor, of Woodbury Miracle Fellowship Center, Inc., your church was a haven for me in a time of transition—thank you!

To the *Who Will Love Me?* team—my nieces and nephew, Garinescia Williams, Matthew Ransom, and Quovadis Wright—thank you for your love, energy, and input with editing this book.

To Pastor Katherine Beckett of Restoring Lives Center, thank you for taking time out of your busy schedule to give your unbiased input in editing portions of this book.

To Pastor Woodrow and Elizabeth Blake, when you blessed me with copies of your books in 2003, it was just what I needed. I then said to myself, "I can do it!"

To Bishop Lee Moore and Lady Louise Moore, thank you for your encouragement and for believing in me.

To Pastor Gracinia Williams-Henry of Solid Rock Christian Ministries, thank you for your longtime friendship and words of encouragement. You gave me clarity and a fresh perspective on my God-given uniqueness.

To Evangelist Marilyn Hann, my longtime friend, thank you for introducing me to my husband, Richard. Together our lives have been enriched.

To Ms. Fay Alice Walker, author of *In Search of … My Brotha, My Lover, My Man* and the president of Favortwou Publishing Company, Inc. and the Georgia Peach Writers: *Who Will Love Me?* has finally become a reality and attending the meetings helped me deliver this baby.

To Bettie J. Jones of B&J Administrative Services, thank you for your service.

To Sarah Hayhurst Editorial, LLC. thank you for your excellent service.

To Minister Donald Hann, thank you for your friendship to Richard and for being a part of our lives.

To Mr. Terence B. Lester, author of *U-Turn*. Thank you for your encouragement.

To Elder Denise Young and Ms. Yvette Gregory, thank you for your encouragement.

To Minister Deon Pennyman, thank you for dedicating your time and support when I first started writing this book.

To Miss Yolanda Goodrum, thank you for believing and investing in me.

To Mrs. LaTonya Elliott, thank you for your prayers and believing in me.

To Elder Bessie Ellis, thank you for your listening ears and caring heart in my time of need.

To Mrs. Sonya Jackson, thank you for your support and prayers.

To Sister Muriel J Kearney, thank you for meeting me at the Walmart. Thank you for your words of wisdom and counsel. Without you, I would not have made it through my first years of marriage.

To Minister Christopher Price, your words, "Let him do it," kept me encouraged, and Evangelist Wanda Petty, thank you for your encouragement that continued to push me forward.

To Ms. Sandra Jones, thank you for sowing into my life. I am so glad you are part of my destiny.

To Mrs. Crystal Bankston, thank you for your support.

To Mrs. Marie Johnson, Mrs. Tracy Wilson-Pyant, and Ms. Beverly Brown, thank you. In reading my manuscript, you gave me your much-needed, constructive input at the beginning of this book.

SPECIAL ACKNOWLEDGMENT

I am thankful for the late founder and pastor of Rock Cathedral Holiness Church, Carrie Johnson and Pastor Frances Williams for carrying on the vision. Their spiritual guidance gave me a strong foundation in loving Jesus Christ and people. They taught me the importance of standing on God's Word, which has been of great value throughout my journey.

Finally, I am grateful for my aunt and uncle the late Reverend Elizabeth C. Few a pioneer in the gospel for women ministers in an unpopular time and Minister Arthur C. Campbell who ensured that his family received the good news of the gospel. They both were spiritual pillars in our family.

I cherish their memories.

DEDICATION

This book is dedicated to my sisters, Mrs. Vincenthes (Tina) Nation, Elder Lachion Morgan, and Ms. Renada Adams; my two brothers-in-law, Billy Nation and Robert Morgan; and to my loving nieces, nephews, aunts, uncle, cousins and my bonus children and their families. Thank you for all your support and for believing in me. This book was written with you in mind.

No matter what you go through in life, Jesus's love is unconditional. He will meet you at your point of need and heal you in your broken places. If you do not know Him as your Lord and Savior, I encourage you to ask Him to come into your heart. I offer Jesus, the only hope for the world today. What the Lord has done for me, He will also do for you. He is not a respecter of persons. Be a living example of Christ in word and in deed because in doing so, your children's children will benefit greatly.

Finally, yet importantly, my brothers and sisters in Christ:

> I am convinced *and* confident of this very thing, that He who has begun a good work in you will [continue to] perfect *and* complete it until the day of Christ Jesus [the time of His return]." (Philippians 1:6)

Be encouraged!

DISCLAIMER

Who Will Love Me? was written from my personal experiences and from others who have shared their experiences with me. This is not the answer to *all* situations. My intention is to share my story to inspire others and bring awareness to the many emotions and inner hurts surrounding people who have a deep need for love and acceptance. This need is not unusual; it is a natural desire that God has placed within us to love and to be loved. With this need, sometimes we can fall prey and become a victim of abuse at many levels. Unfortunately, even onlookers who witness abuse can feel powerless and refuse to acknowledge and speak out against the abuse for fear of rejection and the consequences that may follow.

We were made in the image of God. He is a relational God and has designed the proper order of our love and devotion.

> Jesus said, "The first of all the commandments *is:* 'Hear, O Israel, the Lord our God, the Lord is one. And you shall love the Lord your God with all your heart, with all your soul, with all your mind, and with all your strength.' This is the first commandment. And the second, like it, is this: 'You shall love your neighbor as yourself.' There is no other commandment greater than these." (Mark 12:29–31 NKJV)

Sometimes it may not be easy for a person to recognize when they have fallen prey to an abuser. If you are being abused physically, emotionally, verbally, or mentally or if you are a victim of neglect, seek help!

Be determined and do not stop until you get help! You can be empowered and set free from the strongholds that bind you. You can start with your church if they have counseling services or programs available. Do not stop there until you get help!

However, if you have come to recognize that you are an abuser and cause pain to others, you can change—but you must seek help. An abuser can be a male or female who has an advantage over another person and who can misuse his or her advantage of age, authority, money, or position to hurt and manipulate others.

If you are a substance abuser of alcohol and drugs, there are many programs in place that can help you. As forestated, you can start with your church if they have counseling services or programs available. Do not stop until you get the help you need!

Printed in the United States
By Bookmasters